D1029214

The
Revolutionary War

VOLUME 2

The Revolutionary War

VOLUME 2

The Shot Heard around the World

James R. Arnold & Roberta Wiener

GROLIER
EDUCATIONAL

**First American edition published in 2002
by Grolier Educational**

© 2001 by Graham Beehag Books

Grolier Educational,
90 Sherman Turnpike,
Danbury, Connecticut 06816

Website address: http://publishing.grolier.com

Library of Congress Cataloging-in-Publication Data

The Revolutionary War.
    p. cm.
  Contents: v. 1. The road to rebellion—v. 2. The shot heard around the world—v. 3. Taking up arms—v. 4. The spirit of 1776—v. 5. 1777: a year of decision—v. 6. the road to Valley Forge—v. 7. War of attrition—v. 8. The American cause in peril—v. 9. The turn of the tide —v. 10. An independent nation.
    Includes bibliographical references and indexes.
    ISBN 0-7172-5553-0 (set)—ISBN 0-7172-5554-9 (v. 1)—
ISBN 0-7172-5555-7 (v. 2)—ISBN 0-7172-5556-5 (v. 3)—
ISBN 0-7172-5557-3 (v. 4)—ISBN 0-7172-5558-1 (v. 5)—
ISBN 0-7172-5559-X (v. 6)—ISBN 0-7172-5560-3 (v. 7)—
ISBN 0-7172-5561-1 (v. 8)—ISBN 0-7172-5562-X (v. 9)—
ISBN 0-7172-5563-8 (v. 10)
    1. United States—History—Revolution, 1775–1783—Juvenile literature. [1. united States—History—Revolution. 1775–1783.]
I. Grolier Incorporated.

E208 .R.47 2002
973.3—dc21   2001018998

Printed and bound in Singapore

CONTENTS

CHAPTER ONE

On the Eve of War

The winter of 1774-75 proved a hard time for the British garrison in Boston.

The redcoats and the loyalists were short of food and surrounded by unfriendly people. A British soldier described sailing to Boston around that time. His ship got lost in a storm. The crew saw an American ship and tried to approach to ask for help. When only 300 yards away, the American ship saw "there were Soldiers on board" and "immediately made sail from us and would not have anything to say to us. We supposed she belonged to Boston, as they are remarkable for their [dislike of] people with red coats on."

The Provincial Congress of Massachusetts continued to meet during this time of tension. This was illegal according to the recent British law against town meetings, but delegates met anyway. They formed a Committee of Safety headed by John Hancock. The committee had the power to call out the Massachusetts **militia**. But the committee knew that the militia might not gather in time to meet an emergency. So it organized a special group of militia who could quickly respond. Someone gave them the name "Minutemen" because they could answer the alarm call within a few minutes.

The music of fifes and drums began to sound in towns and villages throughout Massachusetts. Nearby New Hampshire and Rhode Island also organized militias. So did Connecticut, Delaware, Maryland, and Virginia. In all of these colonies militia gathered

A New Army's Growing Pains

Creating a new army is hard. A Connecticut soldier named David Welsh was at Fort Ticonderoga. He wrote to Governor Jonathan Trumbull of Connecticut, on August 5, 1775, to describe some of the problems:

"The men at this place, belonging to the Colony of Connecticut, think they are not well used, as they were promised several things, they don't think there are any steps taken to fulfil it... .

"Several of the companies have no brass kettles to this day. About a week ago I got one for my company, and don't think I shall have any more this year. Pails and bottles we can't get as yet; and not more than one tenth part of the bowls we were to have.... Several companies have no frying-pans... .

"Our water here is very bad and unwholesome, and a great part of the time there is nothing else for the Troops. At present we have some beer but it won't last long.... Rum and molasses are wanted. The rum that comes, as far as I have seen, is worse than none....I think there has not been one pound of soap brought for the Army....

"I am informed that the Continental Congress are to give out commissions; if they do, unless it is well looked to, there will be a great number of officers, and but a few soldiers."

Above: John Hancock served as president of the Massachusetts Provincial Congress and as chairman of the Committee of Safety. He and Sam Adams were the two patriots the British government most wanted to arrest.

Opposite: The people of Boston did not like the British soldiers. Because of their red uniforms, they called them "redcoats" and "lobster backs." Sometimes they called them "bloody backs" because British officers punished them by ordering them whipped, or flogged until their backs bled.

militia: a group of citizens not normally part of the army that mobilises for the purpose of defending the homeland in an emergency; also used as a plural to describe several such groups

desert: to leave the army or navy without permission

so they could practice military training, or drill. Veterans of the French and Indian War taught the militia how to move in military formations and how to use their weapons.

If there was to be a battle, the **militia** would need weapons and gunpowder. In Massachusetts patriots began to steal muskets, and even cannons, from the British. Patriots delighted in getting soldiers drunk and then encouraging them to **desert**. They also traded money, or more often rum, for the soldiers' weapons. It became such a problem that British officers had to

Throughout the colonies the militia prepared for war. Here Pennsylvania riflemen gather for target practice at an event called a rifle frolic. Drinking and socializing were big parts of a rifle frolic.

Right: Paul Revere rode to warn John Sullivan in New Hampshire that the British planned to evacuate Fort William and Mary.

Below: History does not judge Gage kindly. Americans say he was a villain for doing his job too well. Englishmen say he was a poor general for not doing his job well enough.

order ferocious punishments. Soldiers found guilty of selling the weapons received 500 lashes with a heavy whip.

Annoying the British was risky. A militiaman named Thomas Ditson came to Boston. He was caught while trying to buy a musket from a soldier. A group of soldiers tarred and feathered Ditson and drove him from town.

In nearby New Hampshire Major John Sullivan had just returned from the First Continental Congress. He led a group of New Hampshire militia against a British fort at Portsmouth. There were only a few British guards at the fort. Sullivan and his men

disarmed them and stole a large and valuable supply of ammunition.

The most important man in Massachusetts in 1775 was General Thomas Gage. He was both the royal governor and the commander of the British army in North America. He was the official link between King George III and Massachusetts.

Gage was 56 years old in 1775. As a young man he had fought in major battles in Europe. Then he served in America under Braddock during the French and Indian War. At the Battle of the Monongahela River he had shown great courage. Wounded twice, he formed the troops who covered the retreat of the British and American survivors.

Later in the war Gage organized provincial soldiers into the Crown's first regiment of **light infantry**. By that action Gage showed that he understood fighting in the American wilderness. Gage served as military governor of Montreal at the end of the war. Then he moved to New York to become commander-in-chief of the army in North America. Gage did well in that job. At the time, he was well liked by the Americans and trusted by the king.

Gage was at home with his family in England when Parliament passed the Boston Port Bill. The government sent him back to Boston to make the new policy work. Everyone knew that Boston was the center of rebel activity. Everyone knew that Gage's task would be difficult.

Gage hoped that the pressure from the Boston Port Bill would force Boston to change its ways. He was against using military force since it very well might lead to violence. But Gage had a spy who was a delegate to the Massachusetts Committee of Safety. The spy's name was Dr. Benjamin Church. The other members of the Committee of Safety had no idea that Church was a spy. They trusted Church and often listened to his advice. At the end of almost every meeting Church sent a report to General Gage to tell him about the committee's plans.

Church informed Gage that the Massachusetts militia was growing stronger. Gage decided that he had to do something. On February 26, 1775, he sent Colonel Thomas Leslie with some soldiers to the Massachusetts port of Salem. Leslie's mission was to destroy any military supplies he found.

The March to Salem

Leslie landed his men five miles from Salem. As they marched toward the port, an American rider approached. Leslie believed the man was a loyalist. In fact, he was on the rebel side. He rode through the British column and galloped into Salem to alert the citizens.

The townspeople were in church when they heard the news. The local militia commander, Colonel Timothy Pickering, sent 40 Minutemen to a nearby iron forge to

light infantry: a special, or elite, group of foot soldiers chosen for its ability to move and think quickly

British soldiers used the Quartering Act to house soldiers in Boston's Faneuil Hall. Bostonians did not like this.

remove some valuable cannons. Then the townspeople lifted the drawbridge to prevent the redcoats from crossing the North River into Salem. They also moved or destroyed the nearby boats.

Leslie's soldiers arrived at the bridge. What happened

13

Left: Salem, Massachusetts, seen here as it is today, was a busy port until the British closed down all trade because of the Boston Tea Party.

next is confusing. Colonel Leslie reported one set of events. The patriots reported a very different story. What is certain is that the provincial story was believed by the people of Massachusetts.

That account reported that the redcoats arrived at the bridge just as a patriot was destroying the last boat. His name was Joseph Wicher, or Wichener. Wicher

Colonel Leslie behaved cautiously. A more aggressive British officer might have pushed ahead. In that case the first battle of the war might have taken place in Salem.

Paul Revere

Paul Revere, born in 1735, was the son of a Boston silversmith and one of thirteen children. He followed in his father's footsteps and became a silversmith also. Because Boston had so many silversmiths, Paul Revere did other types of work, such as making engravings, drawing political cartoons, and making surgical instruments and false teeth. Even so, his silver work was considered the best in the country.

In addition to his famous ride before the battles of Lexington and Concord, Revere made many other rides to carry the news of important events both before and during the Revolutionary War. He also took part in the Boston Tea Party. He was one of the men dressed as Indians who tossed cases of tea into Boston Harbor. During the war he built a mill and produced gunpowder.

Revere and his first wife had eight children before she died. He then married again and had eight more children. After the war Revere built a factory to make sheet copper. His copper was used to sheathe the famous warship, the *U.S.S. Constitution.* Revere lived to be 83 years old. His ride of April 18, 1775, did not grow into a legend until 1863, when Henry Wadsworth Longfellow wrote a poem called "The Midnight Ride of Paul Revere."

Paul Revere didn't shout, "The British are coming!" Everybody was British in the American colonies of 1775. The warning was that the "regulars" were coming. The regulars referred to the full-time professional soldiers of the British army, who wore the red-coated uniform. Colonists who wanted freedom from Great Britain joined local militia units. They were not regulars, but militiamen, citizen-soldiers who gathered to defend their home soil.

Timothy Pickering served in the Massachusetts militia. He began to study war seriously in 1766 by reading about military history and tactics.

The Salem patriots kept the British from capturing their cannons. The Salem cannons would later prove useful during the Siege of Boston.

dramatically opened his shirt to bare his breast and faced the redcoats. He taunted the soldiers to do something. A British soldier thrust his bayonet into Wicher, giving him a slight, but bloody, wound.

Then British soldiers threatened to open fire against a large group of townspeople and Minutemen who were on the far side of the river. Around that time a woman named Sarah Tarrant is said to have taunted the British from an open window of her home. When soldiers aimed their muskets at her, she is said to have replied, "Fire if you have the courage, but I doubt it."

By all accounts the situation was dangerous. One false step, and fighting would begin. Colonel Leslie was known to be a good man who preferred peace to war. According to the provincial account, a minister and a militia captain suggested a peaceful compromise. The townspeople would lower the bridge to let the soldiers cross. That would allow Leslie to enter Salem. He and his men could keep their honor. But the soldiers could only advance a certain distance before they had to turn back. Leslie accepted the compromise. Just as his men were turning back, militia from nearby towns entered Salem. But they saw the British retreat, and they did not open fire.

The American poet John Trumbull wrote a verse describing the British advance and retreat:

> *Through Salem straight, without delay,*
> *The bold battalion took its way;*
> *Marched o'er a bridge, in open sight*
> *Of several Yankees armed for fight;*
> *Then, without loss of time or men,*
> *Veered round for Boston back again,*
> *And found so well their projects thrive*
> *That every soul got back alive.*

Of course, Leslie's "project," his mission, did not "thrive." Rather, it ended in failure. The Salem militia kept their cannons. Massachusetts patriots learned something from the experience. They decided that the redcoats had orders not to open fire against them. They could annoy the British and even stand in their way

Below: As spring 1775 approached, British soldiers drilled harder. They often practiced firing their muskets at life-sized targets and got into better shape by taking practice marches into the countryside near Boston.

grenadier: a member of a special, or elite, group of infantry soldiers

In addition to his work as a silversmith, engraver, master propagandist, and leader of the Boston Tea Party, Paul Revere was the principal express rider for the Boston Committee of Safety.

without having to worry about their safety. That notion made the militia bold. When the British soldiers marched to Lexington and Concord, the militia would learn that their notion was wrong.

Parliament Passes More Restrictive Laws

Back in England Prime Minister North decided to increase the pressure. North spoke to the House of Commons to build support for his new ideas. He compared the taxes in England and America. He explained that the average tax was fifty times higher in England than in America.

North's speech helped turn Parliament against the Americans. Parliament passed some new acts. Not merely Massachusetts, but all the New England colonies were forbidden to trade with any port except those in England or the British West Indies. That was a very damaging limit on trade. Even worse, Parliament said that the entire New England fishing fleet could not use the North Atlantic fisheries. Those two measures meant that thousands of New England sailors and fishermen would be without jobs.

In Boston another British force made a practice march out from the city. This time it was an entire brigade, numbering nearly a thousand men. Its size took the patriot leaders by surprise. There was no resistance. However, the Massachusetts Provincial Congress decided to be ready if it happened again. It resolved that whenever a British force of 500 men or more left Boston, the militia would be called out. The forces of Massachusetts would stay close to the British but not fight. They would stay "solely on the defensive so long as it can be justified on the Principles of Reason and Self-Preservation and no longer." The British spy, Dr. Church, told Gage this latest news.

On April 14, 1775, General Gage received orders from England. They had been written on January 27, but storms in the Atlantic had delayed the ship carrying the orders. The orders

told Gage to enforce the Acts of Parliament. They recommended arresting Sam Adams and John Hancock. But the orders left it up to Gage to decide exactly what to do.

Gage knew that Adams and Hancock had already left Boston. This made it too difficult to arrest them. From his spy's reports Gage also knew that the Massachusetts militia had stored weapons and supplies in Concord, eighteen miles outside of Boston. So he organized a force to march first to Lexington and then on to Concord. The soldiers' mission was to capture the weapons and supplies.

Patriot Spies and Paul Revere

The patriots inside of Boston learned about this mission because they had formed a spy system. Paul Revere recalled, "In the fall of 1774 and winter of 1775, I was one of upwards of thirty...who formed ourselves into a committee for the purpose of watching the movements of the British soldiers." This group of spies met at the Green Dragon Tavern in Boston. At each meeting each spy swore on the Bible that he would not tell anyone except his own leaders about what they were doing. Each night two pairs of spies patrolled the streets to keep watch. In April 1775 the spies learned that the British had collected boats from the ships in Boston harbor. Then they learned that the best British soldiers, the **grenadier**s and the light infantry, were gathering for a special mission.

The spies passed the information to the Massachusetts Committee of Safety. The committee thought the British goal might be to arrest patriot leaders. Paul Revere rode to Lexington to warn Sam Adams and John Hancock. Revere then returned to Boston. Meanwhile, Lexington passed the warning to Concord. In both towns people

Right: The British grenadiers were the army's best soldiers. They were specially chosen for their courage and size.

A Committee of Safety member prepares the two lanterns to warn of the British crossing Back Bay by boat.

began packing military stores and moving them to safety in the west.

The Committee of Safety knew that there were only two ways for British soldiers to march inland. One was to march over a narrow strip of land, the Boston Neck, that connected Boston with the mainland. The other was to use boats to float across Back Bay and land east of Cambridge. The committee set up a warning system. Spies would watch the British carefully. Once they figured out which way the British were moving, they would send a messenger to the Old North Church. Then a patriot would signal with lanterns from the tall steeple of the church. If he lighted one lantern, it meant that the British would march over the Boston Neck. In other

words, they were moving by land. If he lighted two lanterns, it meant the British were crossing Back Bay by boat, moving by sea. One if by land, two if by sea.

On the night of April 18, 1775, General Gage gave orders to Lieutenant-Colonel Smith. They read:

"Having received Intelligence, that a Quantity of Ammunition, Provision, Artillery, Tents and small Arms, have been collected at Concord, for the Avowed [spoken] Purpose of raising and supporting a Rebellion against His Majesty, you will March with the Corps of Grenadiers and Light Infantry...to Concord."

Gage told Smith to seize or destroy all military goods. He did not tell Smith exactly what to do if the militia showed up to block the redcoats.

Yet, General Gage knew what might happen. Before the march began, he wrote about militia tactics. The

Revere and other post riders often used handbills to spread news among the towns around Boston.

21

militia would act as small "parties of Bushmen," by which he meant that they would hide in the bushes and trees. They were very comfortable using their muskets "and suppose themselves sure of their mark [target]" at long ranges. If a battle began, the militia "would swarm to the place of action" and fight with "wild" enthusiasm. Gage's prediction was correct.

The grenadier and light infantry companies formed on Boston Common at dusk. They numbered about 700 fighting men. They rowed across the water toward Cambridge. They waded ashore and waited for extra food (called rations) to arrive. They waited for two cold, uncomfortable hours. Between 1 A.M. and 2 A.M. the march began. Most of the soldiers did not want to carry the extra weight, so they threw their rations into the nearby marsh!

Colonel Smith led the column to a bridge. He wanted to avoid making noise. So Smith had the men cross

Paul Revere's house in Boston

Paul Revere looks back toward the Old North Church to see the signal that the British are moving by sea.

over a ford rather than use the bridge. Smith need not have bothered. The Americans already knew that he was coming.

Spies had seen Smith gather his men on Boston Common. A patriot woke Paul Revere to tell him that the British were moving! Members of the spy group led Revere past the British guard posts. They took him to a boat so he could cross the Charles River. They had to be very careful since their boat passed just behind a British warship, the *Somerset*. It was about 10 P.M., and a bright moon was rising. Revere looked back toward Boston. Two lanterns glowed in the spire of Old North Church. This signal meant that the British were moving by sea.

The task for Revere and another rider, William Dawes, was to ride through the countryside to warn people that the British soldiers, or regulars, were coming. This would cause the Minutemen and the militia to assemble. Revere's main mission was also to ride to Lexington to warn again Hancock and Adams. Revere and Dawes knew that somewhere out in the dark there were British riders whose mission was to prevent anyone from spreading the alarm. So they knew that they would have to be careful.

Revere began his ride. He soon saw two British riders. Revere galloped away to safety. He rode through Medford, where he alerted the captain of the Minutemen. He rode toward

Opposite Below:
"A voice in the darkness, a knock at the door,
And a word that shall echo forevermore!
For, borne on the night-wind of the Past,
Through all our history, to the last,
In the hour of darkness and peril and need,
The people will waken and listen to hear
The hurrying hoof-beats of that steed,
And the midnight message of Paul Revere."

Below:
"A hurry of hoofs in a village street,
A shape in the moonlight, a bulk in the dark . . .
Through the gloom and the light,
The fate of the nation was riding that night."

Above: John Hancock and Sam Adams were sleeping in this house in Lexington when Paul Revere arrived to warn them.

Lexington, shouting out his warning to every house and farm. Dawes rode along a different route and did the same. Revere reached Lexington around midnight. There he found Minutemen already assembled to guard the house where Adams and Hancock were staying. These Minutemen had seen British riders and figured out on their own that something unusual was taking place. So they gathered to guard the two important leaders.

Revere said he wanted to speak to Adams and Hancock. Sergeant William Munroe replied that the family had gone to bed and had asked "that they might not be disturbed by any noise about the house."

"Noise!" replied Revere. "You'll have noise enough before long. The regulars are coming out."

CHAPTER TWO

Lexington and Concord

The British march to Concord led to the first battle of the American Revolution.

A messenger riding a pony to Lexington, carrying a warning letter from Dr. Warren to John Hancock.

Right: Before the British arrived in Lexington, the alarm had spread wide.

Before Paul Revere arrived in Lexington, the Lexington militia did not know if the British regulars were coming. Revere persuaded Sergeant Munroe to let him warn Adams and Hancock. Then Revere prepared to keep going. William Dawes joined him, and together the two riders set off for nearby Concord. They made it halfway there. About 1:30 A.M. they ran into a British patrol. Dawes escaped back to Lexington. Revere was captured.

The two riders had had enough time to do their job. Word spread quickly and alerted the country-side. The Minutemen and militia were gathering at their posts.

Meanwhile, the British column marched slowly on. To move more rapidly, Smith ordered Major John Pitcairn to go ahead with six companies of light infantry. He also sent word to Gage that the provincials had sounded the alarm. He asked Gage to send reinforcements. That

Major Pitcairn was like most British officers in Boston. He believed that the provincials had gone too far with their protest. He thought a firm hand would stop the disorder and bring back respect for king and Parliament. Legend has it that Pitcairn stopped for a morning drink at a tavern. He stirred it with his fingers and said, "I mean to stir the Yankee blood as I stir this before night."

The Wright Tavern where Pitcairn paused for a drink.

turned out to be a very wise request.

In Lexington Captain John Parker had assembled about 130 Minutemen. But when no regulars appeared, Parker decided it was a false alarm. He sent most of his men to bed with orders to return if they heard the beating of a signal drum. Parker also sent four scouts down the Boston road.

A small group of British soldiers marched at the front of Pitcairn's column. Their job was to move quietly and find any enemy. They heard Parker's scouts approaching. The British captured the first three scouts. The fourth scout was Thaddeus Brown. Brown's horse either heard or smelled the hidden British. It stopped. This saved Brown from capture. Brown saw that the regulars had come and galloped back to Lexington. He warned Parker that the British were only half a mile away. It was about 4:30 in the morning.

Only about seventy of Parker's Minutemen had ammunition. Parker formed them in the middle of the village on open ground called the Lexington Green. Just as the sun was rising, Pitcairn and his light infantry appeared. Pitcairn ordered his men to form a line. The redcoats cheered as they ran into position. This scared some of the Minutemen, and they began to move away from the British soldiers. Parker ordered his men to stand fast.

Pitcairn was not worried about the little force of Minutemen. He ordered them to lay down their weapons. Parker saw that it was hopeless to fight. He ordered his men to retreat. Then someone fired a shot. Which side fired first is unknown. Several other shots rang out. A British officer ordered his unit to fire. The redcoats fired at a range of about 40 yards. Then they charged.

A few patriots fired back. Most broke and ran. Parker's cousin Jonas stood his ground even though he was wounded. He was trying to reload his musket when a British soldier thrust his bayonet. Jonas Parker died from the blow. In just a few minutes it was over. Eight Americans lay dead and 10 wounded. Only one redcoat received a light wound.

The British passed through Lexington and on toward

Opposite: The first clash in Lexington. Major Pitcairn is mounted at the front of his men.

Below: On April 19, 1775, a column of British soldiers set out to Lexington and Concord. Paul Revere and William Dawes alerted the American minutemen and militia. They gathered to fight the British. The first clash came at Lexington. The British continued to Concord. Here they met increasing numbers of angry rebels. During the British retreat back to Boston, the rebels made many fierce attacks.

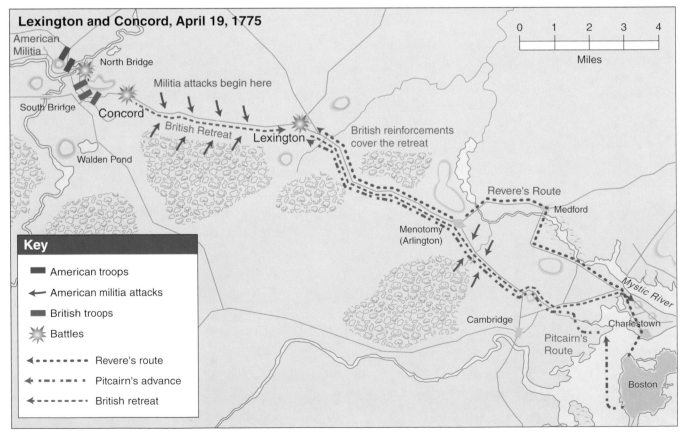

Lexington and Concord, April 19, 1775

Below: Parker is said to have told his men, "Don't fire unless fired upon. But if they mean to have a war, let it begin here!" In fact, Parker probably only told his men to hold firm.

Concord, six miles away. In Concord a small force of militia had gathered. They were trying to carry off or hide the military supplies when the redcoats appeared. It was about 7 A.M. The militia did not resist. They retreated across North Bridge and waited for reinforcements.

The British did not yet realize how many militia were gathering. At least 75 militia companies lived within five miles of the road used by the British to march to Concord. This meant that the British would soon be outnumbered about four to one. A trap was forming. The militia began moving toward Concord from all directions.

In and around Concord the British soldiers searched for the military supplies.

A realistic painting showing Parker's men and British soldiers trading shots.

They did not find very much. During this time the soldiers behaved respectfully toward the civilians. Soldiers set fire to the military supplies. The fire spread to a nearby building. The British quickly put it out.

Near North Bridge one group of Minutemen saw the smoke rising from Concord. They thought that the British were burning the town. Their commander spoke. A Minuteman recalled that the officer "said if we were all of his mind we would drive them from the bridge....We all said we would go."

The Minutemen advanced toward the bridge with drums beating. Captain Isaac Davis and his company led the way. Later his wife remembered: "My husband said but little that morning. He seemed serious and thoughtful; but he never seemed to hesitate as to the course of his duty. As he led the company from the house, he turned himself round

The Minutemen and militia quickly gathered to march toward Lexington and Concord.

32

The militia charge over North Bridge marked the beginning of the British disaster.

Below: The militia, the citizen-soldiers of Massachusetts, left their homes to fight the British.

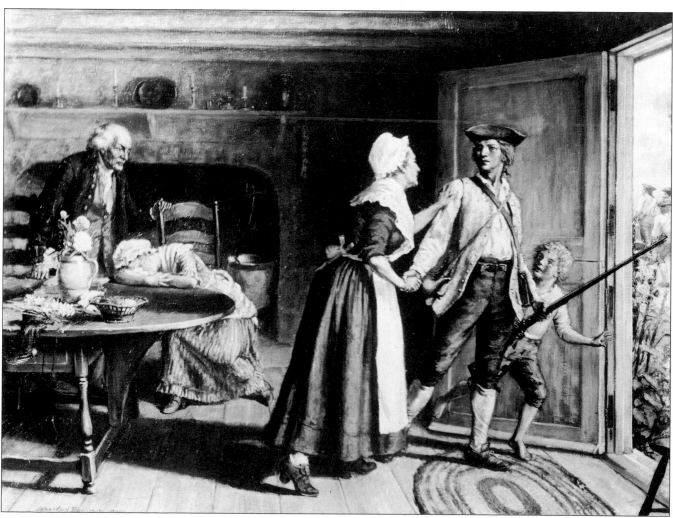

and said 'Take good care of the children,' and was soon out of sight."

British soldiers waited for Davis and his men on the far side of the bridge. Since there had already been fighting in Lexington, the redcoats did not hesitate to fire first. A bullet hit Isaac Davis in the chest and killed him. This time the Americans stood their ground and fired back. A three-minute exchange took place. The Americans' heavy fire drove the redcoats back in disorder. Three British soldiers died, and eight received wounds. Two Americans were killed and three were wounded.

The Americans drove the British back into Concord. One militiaman used a hatchet to chop at the head of a British soldier while he lay helpless on the ground. The other British soldiers became very angry when they learned about it. The word spread that the provincials

The action at North Bridge by a famous battle painter, Alonzo Chappel.

were scalping the fallen British. The redcoats would take their revenge soon.

Around noon the British commander, Colonel Smith, ordered his men to march back to Boston. They covered the first mile without difficulty. But hundreds of Minutemen and militia had turned out. As the British came to a bridge, the Americans opened a heavy fire.

At first the retreating soldiers were not too worried. Then they began to suffer casualties. Most of them were young soldiers, new to war. They had been taught that if they kept their formation and fired quickly, they could win. But the Americans were hard targets to hit, and the young soldiers tended to fire when they were too far away. Such long-range fire was not very dangerous to the militia. Once the militia sensed this, they became bolder. Their fire became heavier. The grenadiers and light infantry took more and more losses.

The British soldiers endured this fire for the rest of the march. The Americans fought "Indian style." They hid behind walls, trees, and buildings on both sides of the road

When the British began to retreat from Concord, the militia closed in like wolves attacking a wounded animal.

35

and fired when a target appeared. The British light infantry moved on both sides, or flanks, of the road. Sometimes they could catch the militia. When they did, they killed them.

Smith had asked for reinforcements. Lord Percy led another 1,400 redcoats and two cannons to Lexington. There, at about 2:30, the retreating grenadiers and light infantry saw them. They greeted Percy's men with a cheer. They correctly believed that they were saved. Indeed, if Percy had not come when he did, the

grenadiers and light infantry almost certainly would have been destroyed.

One of Percy's soldiers described what he heard and saw as he approached Lexington: "As we advanced we heard the firing plainer and more frequent....We could observe a Considerable number of the Rebels, but they were much scattered, and not above 50 of them to be seen in a body in any place. Many lay concealed behind the Stone walls and fences."

The British showed great courage during the retreat.

The militia continued to annoy the retreating British. Some came so close that the redcoats could hear their shouts. Instead of "God Save the King," they called out the name of one of their own leaders, "King Hancock forever!" A British soldier described the tactics used by the militia. They: "Always posted themselves in the houses and behind the walls by the roadside, and there waited the approach of the Column, when they fired at it. Numbers of them were mounted, and when they had fastened their horses at some little distance from the road, they crept down near enough to have a Shot; as soon as the Column had passed, they mounted again and rode round until they got ahead of the Column, and found some convenient place from whence they might fire again. These fellows were generally good marksmen."

Other militia shot at the British from the shelter of nearby houses. Lord Percy ordered his men to burn these houses. The British officers were already losing control

The Massachusetts militia believed that they were defending their homes from a foreign invader.

Opposite: A British officer orders a retreat from the bridge at Concord.

Slowly British discipline collapsed, and soldiers began burning and looting.

of their men. The soldiers had heard about the defenseless soldier whom the Americans had killed. The sight of burning houses made things worse. It was like a signal saying discipline was ended. They broke from the ranks to enter nearby homes. If they found any men inside, they bayoneted them. If they found the house empty, they stole the valuables.

The militia chased the redcoats all the way back to Charlestown Neck. At dusk the tired, battered British returned to their lines. Once the redcoats arrived there, they were safe.

propaganda: information presented in a way to convince people of a certain point of view

CHAPTER THREE

After the Battle

The Battle of Lexington and Concord changed everything.

The British garrison of Boston awoke the day after the battle to find themselves in a war. They guarded Boston and waited for an attack.

Meanwhile, the military surgeons began caring for the wounded. The way they did this was very different from modern medicine. They had no idea about germs, no idea about the importance of cleanliness. They had no good drugs to give.

They often began their care by bleeding—making a cut to draw blood from—the injured men. They did not give them food because it was believed that food was bad for a wounded man. They could set broken bones. They could cut off, or amputate, badly damaged arms or legs.

Opposite: Patriotic printers published the names of the Massachusetts men who died during the Battle of Lexington and Concord.

Below: After the battle the pastor at Lexington gave a sermon. He said that the British were "more like murderers and cut-throats than the troops of a Christian king [for no reason] without warning, when no war was proclaimed, they draw the sword of violence upon the inhabitants of this town, and with a cruelty and barbarity which would have made the most innocent savage blush, they shed INNOCENT BLOOD!"

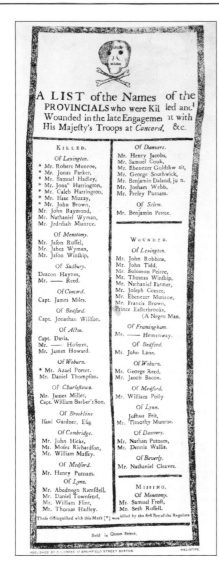

A LIST of the Names of the PROVINCIALS who were Killed and Wounded in the late Engagement with His Majesty's Troops at *Concord*, &c.

KILLED.

Of Lexington.
* Mr. Robert Munroe,
* Mr. Jonas Parker,
* Mr. Samuel Hadley,
* Mr. Jon^a Harrington,
* Mr. Caleb Harrington,
* Mr. Isaac Muzzy,
* Mr. John Brown,
Mr. John Raymond,
Mr. Nathaniel Wyman,
Mr. Jedediah Munroe.

Of Menotomy.
Mr. Jason Russel,
Mr. Jabez Wyman,
Mr. Jason Winship.

Of Sudbury.
Deacon Haynes,
Mr. —— Reed.

Of Concord.
Capt. James Miles.

Of Bedford.
Capt. Jonathan Willson.

Of Acton.
Capt. Davis,
Mr. —— Hosmer,
Mr. James Howard.

Of Woburn.
* Mr. Azael Porter,
Mr. Daniel Thompson.

Of Charlestown.
Mr. James Miller,
Capt. William Barber's Son.

Of Brookline
Isaac Gardner, Esq.

Of Cambridge.
Mr. John Hicks,
Mr. Moses Richardson,
Mr. William Massey.

Of Medford.
Mr. Henry Putnam.

Of Lynn.
Mr. Abednego Ramsdell,
Mr. Daniel Townsend,
Mr. William Flint,
Mr. Thomas Hadley.

Of Danvers.
Mr. Henry Jacobs,
Mr. Samuel Cook,
Mr. Ebenezer Goldthwait,
Mr. George Southwick,
Mr. Benjamin Daland, ju n.
Mr. Jotham Webb,
Mr. Perley Putnam.

Of Salem.
Mr. Benjamin Peirce.

WOUNDED.

Of Lexington.
Mr. John Robbins,
Mr. John Tidd,
Mr. Solomon Peirce,
Mr. Thomas Winship,
Mr. Nathaniel Farmer,
Mr. Joseph Comee,
Mr. Ebenezer Munroe,
Mr. Francis Brown,
Prince Easterbrooks,
    (A Negro Man.

Of Framingham.
Mr. —— Hemenway.

Of Bedford.
Mr. John Lane.

Of Woburn.
Mr. George Reed,
Mr. Jacob Bacon.

Of Medford.
Mr. William Polly.

Of Lynn.
Joshua Felt,
Mr. Timothy Munroe.

Of Danvers.
Mr. Nathan Putnam,
Mr. Dennis Wallis.

Of Beverly.
Mr. Nathaniel Cleaves.

MISSING.

Of Menotomy.
Mr. Samuel Frost,
Mr. Seth Russell.

Those distinguished with this Mark [*] were killed by the first fire of the Regulars.

Sold in Queen Street.

PUBLISHED BY S. G. DRAKE 17 BROMFIELD STREET BOSTON.   HELIOTYPE.

After that, they could only wait and see what happened. Soldiers knew that going to the hospital was very dangerous. Many tried to stay away even though they were badly hurt.

It was a hard time for the soldiers' wives. One wife knew that her wounded husband had been left behind and captured. She wrote: "My husband is now lying in one of their [the American] hospitals...and there are now forty or fifty thousand of them [the militia] gathered together; and we are not four thousand at most. It is a very troublesome time for we are expecting the town to be burnt down every day, I believe we are [lost], and I hear my husband's leg is broke, and my heart is almost broken."

Until the battle on April 19, 1775, patriots had annoyed the king's soldiers but never shot at them. Until now the redcoats had taken the American abuse but, except in the case of the Boston Massacre, had not used their weapons to defend themselves. After April 19 the patriots and the redcoats were enemies.

April 19 gave the radicals just what they needed. They quickly wrote a description of what had happened. It was addressed to "All Friends of American Liberty." It was not quite a true account. It made special mention of some events and ignored others. This type of part true and part false report is called propaganda. Patriot writers were very good at making propaganda.

Fast-riding messengers carried the **propaganda** about the battles at Lexington and Concord. One rider spread the news across Connecticut and reached New York City on April 23. He then continued through New Jersey to Philadelphia. Other men, called express riders, rode day and night to carry a more complete account. They came to New York on April 25 and made it all the way to Charleston, South Carolina, by May 10.

Patriot leaders knew about the battle within three weeks. That was a very quick movement of news for the time. Of course, it took longer for the news to cross the Atlantic. Massachusetts patriots, including Joseph Warren, wanted their report of the battle, their propaganda, to reach England first. They hired a fast sailing ship. It left Salem on April 28 and arrived in England four weeks later.

In Roman history Cincinnatus was called from his farm to save Rome from its enemies. After winning, Cincinnatus returned to his farm. The Minutemen viewed Cincinnatus as their model. This painting in the U.S. Capitol shows Cincinnatus being called from his farm.

The news upset some Englishmen. The king reacted calmly. He saw that the American report was propaganda, "drawn up with the intention of painting a skirmish at Concord in as favorable light as possible" for the rebels.

Gage's official report came twelve days later. It too was not quite truthful. In fact, his army had lost 73 killed and 174 wounded. However, Gage reported "above 50 killed and many more wounded."

Gage was more honest in a private letter. There he showed that the battle had taught him a lesson. He wrote how the rebels had fought hard and well. They showed themselves to be much better than they had been back in the French and Indian War. If officials in England thought a war would be easy, they were making a mistake: "the conquest of this country is not easy." It would take strong armies willing to fight stubbornly for a long time.

No British official really listened to Gage's wise words. Later, people could see the importance of Lexington and Concord. At the time, the king and his government did not realize how important they were.

Back in Boston, Lord Percy wrote his report the day

after the battle. He knew that most British officers had shared his own thought that the provincials would be poor soldiers. Just as it did Gage, the battle taught Percy a lesson: "Whoever looks upon them as an irregular mob, will find himself much mistaken. They have men amongst them who know very well what they are about, having been employed as Rangers against the Indians and Canadians, and this country being much covered with wood, and hilly, is very advantageous for their method of fighting."

The day after the battle the Massachusetts Committee of Safety sent a letter to all of Massachusetts. It asked the towns to help form an army quickly. Massachusetts answered the call. An army gathered outside of Boston and surrounded the city.

For most of next the two months there was little fighting. Militia men and redcoats shot at one another, but they most often missed. Both sides seemed to be waiting to see what would happen next.

Below: In 1775 legend has it that a rider found Israel Putnam plowing a field. When the rider told Putnam about the fighting, he stopped working, mounted his plow horse, and rode toward Boston. This painting is also from the U.S. Capitol. By showing Cincinnatus and Putnam side by side, the paintings show how proper citizen-soldiers behave. After the Revolutionary War American veterans formed the Society of the Cincinnati in honor of the legendary citizen-soldier of Rome. The society still exists today.

CHAPTER FOUR

The Second Continental Congress

The delegates to the Second Continental Congress had to answer a critical question: Should they help Massachusetts in its fight against the British Army?

On May 10, 1775, delegates met at the State House in Philadelphia. Many of them had been at the First Continental Congress. They included John Hancock, John Adams, and George Washington. There were also some new delegates, including Thomas Jefferson of Virginia and Benjamin Franklin of Pennsylvania.

Below: The Second Continental Congress held a historic, important meeting in Philadelphia.

They had much to do. The colonies were not yet at war with England. But in Massachusetts there had already been a battle. The situation was confusing. New York delegates worried about what they would do if a British force appeared in New York Harbor. Delegates said to let the British land peacefully. New Yorkers should fight only in defense of their homes. Just in case, the congress appointed George Washington to study how best to defend New York.

The delegates' most urgent job was to answer a letter from the president of the Massachusetts Provincial Congress, Dr. Joseph Warren. Warren asked for advice and help. He wanted the Continental Congress to form a powerful army and come to the aid of the militia outside of Boston.

Delegates debated how to answer Warren. They voted to have the colonies prepare to defend themselves, but they were not yet ready to do any more. Then came startling news on May 17: Ethan Allen and his Green

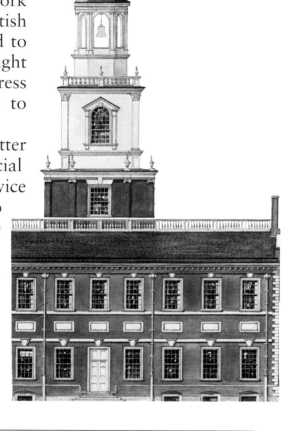

Right: Delegates to the Second Continental Congress met at the Pennsylvania capital building. Later, this building was renamed Independence Hall.

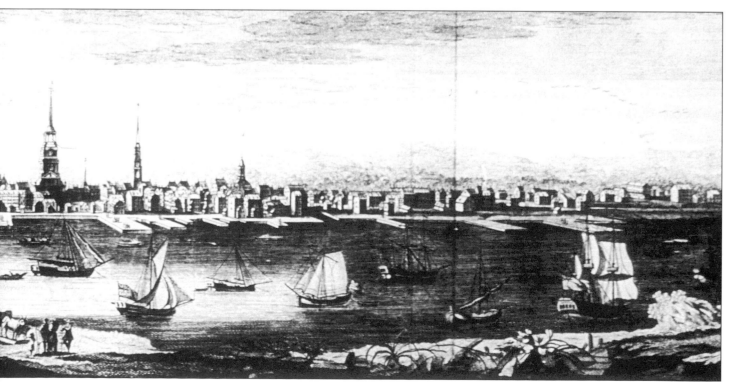

How Soldiers Fought

Combat during the Revolutionary War was very different from modern war.

Most of the soldiers who fought in the Revolutionary War used smoothbore, muzzle-loading, flintlock muskets. British soldiers carried a kind of musket called the "Brown Bess." The Brown Bess was heavy. Each one weighed fourteen pounds. A 16-inch socket bayonet fitted under the barrel. The Brown Bess fired a one-ounce ball. Its maximum range was about 1,000 yards, but no one fired at that range because the musket was too inaccurate. Instead, soldiers waited until a group of men came within 200 yards before they fired. At that range some of the balls could hit the target.

After each shot the soldier had to reload. He took a paper cartridge from his pouch or cartridge box and tore it open. If he was in a hurry, as was the case in most battles, he bit the cartridge open. Biting the cartridge let gunpowder into his mouth. The gunpowder made a soldier very thirsty.

The soldier poured a small amount of gunpowder into the priming pan while the musket's cock was set at the half-cock, or safety position. He rested the musket with its butt end on the ground and poured the rest of the powder into the barrel. The musket ball was spat or dropped into the barrel.

An iron ramrod hung beneath the musket barrel. The soldier took the ramrod to push the paper tube of the cartridge down the barrel until it seated against the breech, or side. The paper formed a wad to hold the ball and powder in place. He replaced the ramrod, pulled the cock to full, and lifted the musket. That was called "presenting," as in "present arms." He rested the musket against his right shoulder. It could not be placed against the left shoulder because the powder in the priming pan, located on the right side of the musket, would burn the left eye.

Soldiers practiced these steps for hours. Such practice was an important part of drilling. Once the soldier learned by memory how to prepare the weapon for firing, he was taught how to aim and fire. Soldiers were taught to fire in groups at the same time. The resulting fire was called a volley. A single shot might fly wild. A volley was more likely to score some hits. Drill taught some men to aim carefully. In the excitement of battle many simply pointed their muskets in the general direction of the enemy.

The soldier squeezed the trigger. The hammer crashed down so the flint struck sparks. The sparks fell on the priming pan. The pan burst into flame. The flame moved into a hole called the touch hole. There the flame met the rest of the powder and exploded it with a loud noise. The ball left the barrel while the musket recoiled hard against the shoulder. The soldier lowered his musket to reload.

Well-trained soldiers could fire about four times a minute until the musket barrel became dirty with unburned powder. Then the rate slowed. Soldiers carried between 30 and 60 rounds of ammunition.

So that everyone could fire, soldiers formed a battle line. Because soldiers needed to fire massed volleys to be effective, they stood very close together. They were so close that their shoulders almost touched, which was called shoulder-to-shoulder formation. An American battle line had soldiers standing two deep. In other words, for each man in the front line or front rank there was another man behind him in the second rank. At the beginning of the war the British fought three ranks deep. Later they changed to fight in two ranks. One rank could stand and fire over the heads of the soldiers in front, who were kneeling and firing.

Behind the formed battle line were the "file closers." Their job was to make sure that the men in front did not run away. When a man was killed or wounded, the file closers herded the survivors closer together in order to keep the battle line in shoulder-to-shoulder formation.

All firearms during the Revolution used black powder ammunition. Black powder made vast amounts of smoke. A line of men who fired their muskets became hidden in their own smoke. The smoke on a battlefield added to a battle's confusion.

Officers usually did not carry muskets. Instead they carried swords. They were usually straight, single-edged weapons. Since most battles were decided by lines of soldiers firing at one another, officers were seldom close enough to an enemy to use their swords.

A typical battle of the Revolutionary War saw the battle lines form 300 to 600 yards apart. Then one or both sides advanced to the beat of the drum and the squealing of the fife. When the lines were 100 yards apart or even closer, the soldiers opened fire. They traded volleys until one side began to weaken.

Then came the order "Fix Bayonets!" Soldiers attached their bayonets to their muskets. Then came the order to charge. The soldiers marched quickly straight at the enemy. It took great discipline to advance into the face of point-blank musket and cannon fire.

The sight of a line of men advancing with fixed bayonets was frightening. No one wanted to be stuck by a sharp bayonet. Soldiers facing a bayonet charge endured the supreme test on a battlefield.

If there were enough defenders who stood firm, they continued to fire massed volleys quickly. Their fire would stop the charge. If the defenders saw that they could not save themselves by firing their muskets, they usually broke and ran before the attackers closed to bayonet them.

If the attackers kept advancing and the defenders stood, a brief hand-to-hand struggle, or melee, took place. Soldiers thrust their bayonets, used their muskets like clubs, kicked, and punched. A melee did not last long. One side or the other could not stand it and would break and run.

It is not natural to stand firm and face this type of horrible fighting. It was the purpose of hours of drill to teach men to stand and fight. Fire discipline, the ability to load, aim, and fire at the word of command, was the most important skill. To win a battle soldiers had to show fire discipline even in the middle of terrible and frightening conditions.

The British regulars were well drilled. Years of training taught them to fire massed volleys very quickly. The redcoats could take heavy losses and continue to fight. They almost always showed good fire discipline. These skills made them famous. These skills also made them very hard to beat.

The American army was a collection of citizen-soldiers. When the war started, there were no regulars. It took time for the Americans to learn the skills needed to fight and win.

Benjamin Franklin was one of the delegates at the Second Continental Congress.

Mountain Boys of Vermont, along with Benedict Arnold of Connecticut, had captured the British fort at Ticonderoga.

Fort Ticonderoga

Ethan Allen lived in what is today the state of Vermont. In 1775 that area was called the New Hampshire Grants. Allen had organized a group of men to resist royal authority. He called them the Green Mountain Boys. They behaved in such a lawless way that some people called them the Bennington Mob.

After Allen heard the news of Lexington and Concord, he wanted to strike a blow for liberty. Allen decided to attack Fort Ticonderoga, the important fortress on Lake Champlain. He did not know that another man, Benedict Arnold, had the same idea.

Arnold lived in Connecticut. When he heard the news of Lexington and Concord, he gathered a few men and rushed to join the Massachusetts forces outside of Boston. The Massachusetts Provincial Congress made Arnold a colonel. Colonel Arnold said he wanted to capture Fort Ticonderoga. The Massachusetts Provincial Congress told him to go ahead and recruit troops to attack the fort. Arnold was an impatient man. He left other men to recruit and rushed to the New Hampshire Grants.

Arnold found Ethan Allen and his men marching toward Fort Ticonderoga. Arnold said that he should command the Green Mountain Boys. The men did not know Arnold and replied no. So Allen continued to lead the Green Mountain Boys while Arnold tagged along.

There were under 50 British soldiers in Fort Ticonderoga on the night of May 10, 1775. General Gage had sent the fort's commander a warning to stay alert. The commander, Captain William Delaplace, had not paid attention. The attack by 83 Green Mountain Boys surprised the soldiers in the fort. Delaplace was asleep. He woke up and did not even have time to dress.

Ethan Allen wakes up the British commander at Fort Ticonderoga.

He went outside to ask in whose name the fort had been broken into.

Ethan Allen is said to have replied, "In the name of the Great Jehovah, and the Continental Congress."

The Green Mountain Boys seized the fort without a fight. They captured a great amount of very useful supplies, including about 85 good pieces of artillery and several tons of cannon and musket balls.

The capture of Fort Ticonderoga presented a problem for the delegates to the Second Continental Congress. In Massachusetts the Americans had been defending themselves. At Fort Ticonderoga the Americans had attacked first.

At first the delegates decided that they should abandon the fort. Delegates from New York and New England protested. During the French and Indian War Fort Ticonderoga had been the key. If the British got it back, they might set the Indians to raiding again. Finally, on May 31 the Congress voted to keep the fort.

Then delegates began moving at a faster pace. On June 3 they voted to raise money to buy gunpowder. On June 14 they voted to raise a Continental Army. Soldiers would be recruited from Pennsylvania, Maryland, and Virginia. They would then march to Boston.

An army needed a commander-in-chief. John Adams and his cousin Samuel knew that New Englanders expected that an army in New England should be commanded by a New Englander. But the Adamses believed that if Congress gave the command to a southerner, that act would help unite the colonies. The

The Second Continental Congress made the important decision to raise a regular, or standing, army.

most important southern colony was Virginia, so the general would have to be a Virginian. The Adamses talked it over with other delegates, and a majority of them agreed. On June 15 they elected George Washington to command all Continental forces "for the defense of American liberty."

George Washington felt honored by the appointment. He was ambitious, and so this high appointment pleased him. It also frightened him. Commander-in-chief was a huge responsibility. He feared that he might fail. He compared the task ahead with taking a voyage across a stormy ocean toward an unknown shore.

The Olive Branch Petition

Even while the Second Continental Congress made preparations for war, delegates still hoped for peace. They wrote a letter to King George. It became known as the Olive Branch Petition because an olive branch was a symbol of peace. The Olive Branch Petition again explained the American view of taxes and liberty. It said that Americans still loved their king. It begged the king to stop the conflict and let everyone solve their disagreements by talking, not fighting.

A firm loyalist named Richard Penn, a descendent of William Penn who founded Pennsylvania, took the Olive Branch Petition to London. The king believed that the Continental Congress was an illegal group. He refused to see Penn or to read the petition.

Meanwhile, George Washington left Philadelphia on a ride to Boston. Before he arrived, another battle had taken place.

Left: John Adams cleverly arranged to have George Washington become the commander of the American army. Many northern delegates did not like southerners. Most felt differently about George Washington. When Washington became commander-in-chief, a New England delegate wrote that he was no "ranting swearing fellow but Sober, steady, and Calm."

CHAPTER FIVE

The Battle of Bunker Hill

*After the fighting at Lexington and Concord the
Massachusetts militia surrounded Boston.*

General Artemas Ward was the commander of the Massachusetts militia. Ward was 48 years old. He had been active in the militia since boyhood. However, he had seen very little war service. He was careful and slow moving. His men trusted him. He had been sick on April 19 at the time the news reached him of the fighting at Lexington and Concord. He rode to Cambridge the next morning to take command.

The patriot force that gathered around Boston was a civilian army, an army of citizen-soldiers. The recruits included a few free blacks, a handful of British deserters, and a company of Stockbridge Indians. They were unlike the professionals in the British army. John Trumbull, the 19-year-old son of the governor of

Massachusetts militia march to the fighting. They are carrying a flag that later came to be called the "Bunker Hill" flag.

Men from nearby colonies marched to join the Massachusetts men at Boston.

Connecticut, described the forces besieging Boston: "The entire army, if it deserved the name, was but [a group] of brave, enthusiastic, undisciplined country lads; the officers in general quite as ignorant of military life as the troops."

By June 9, 1775, there were 11,636 Massachusetts men surrounding Boston. They were in two large groups. One was around Cambridge to guard the Cambridge Neck. The other was around Roxbury to guard the Boston Neck. By guarding these two positions, the Americans prevented the British from marching inland.

When the nearby colonies heard about the fighting at Lexington and Concord, they raised their militia to help. Connecticut sent a force of two regiments numbering about 2,300 men to reinforce the Massachusetts men. New Hampshire sent about 1,500 men.

A force of 1,390 men marched in from Rhode Island. They were the best trained and equipped in the entire army. A very skilled leader named Nathanael Greene led them.

The patriot forces had never worked together before. They suffered from a shortage of equipment, particularly artillery. There were no trained staff, artillerymen, or engineers. The soldiers lacked discipline. The leaders lacked experience.

On May 25, 1775, British reinforcements sailed into Boston Harbor. They included three major-generals who were to play very important roles in the rest of the war: John Burgoyne, Henry Clinton, and William Howe. None of them was a poor general, but none of them was brilliant. They thought of themselves as rivals and did not get along very well. They also did not get along with General Gage. This was important because they needed to cooperate if they were going to lead the army to victory.

New orders for Gage also came on May 25. Gage was told to declare Massachusetts in a state of rebellion. Then he would have to do something to put down the rebellion. Gage and his generals worked out a plan to attack the Americans. American spies learned about the plan and passed the news to the Committee of Safety.

On June 15 the Committee of Safety made its own plan. The committee ordered General Ward to move a force to Bunker Hill. There it would be in a good position to keep the British off the Charlestown Peninsula. The next evening a force of about 1,200 men gathered on the Cambridge Common. The president of Harvard College offered a long prayer for their success and safety.

On the night of June 16 the Americans' inexperience and the lack of staff officers was evident. Bunker Hill stood about 110 feet high. It was a safe position because the British could not move in behind the hill and separate the rebels from the main American army. For reasons that have never been explained, a mistake took

The Americans dug earthworks the night before the Battle of Bunker Hill. They were not professional soldiers and made many mistakes.

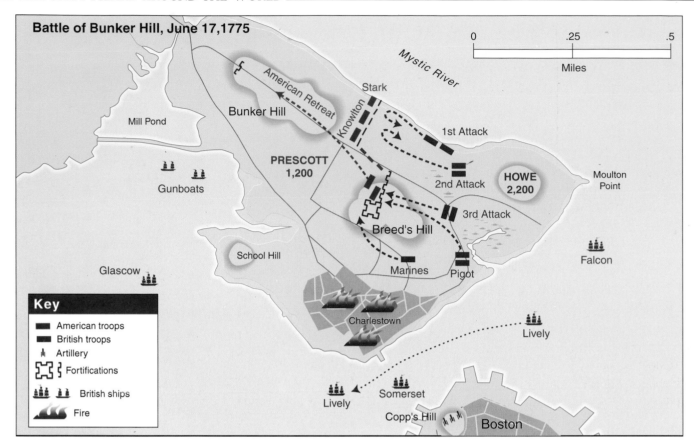

Battle of Bunker Hill, June 17, 1775

0   .25   .5
Miles

Mystic River

Stark

American Retreat

Bunker Hill

Knowlton

1st Attack

Mill Pond

PRESCOTT
1,200

Moulton
Point

2nd Attack

HOWE
2,200

Gunboats

3rd Attack

Breed's Hill

School Hill

Falcon

Glasgow

Marines

Pigot

Key

- ▬ American troops
- ▬ British troops
- ⵑ Artillery
- ⊡ Fortifications
- ⛵ ⛵ British ships
- 🔥 Fire

Charlestown

Lively

Lively

Somerset

Copp's Hill

Boston

place. Most of the rebels marched over Bunker Hill and continued to Breed's Hill.

Breed's Hill rose only 60 feet. It was isolated and easy for the British to bypass. Yet the rebels began digging on Breed's Hill to build a simple fort, or redoubt. They also made a **breastworks** to the left of the redoubt. But there was a gap between the left end of these works and the Mystic River.

The next morning General Gage awoke to the sound of cannon fire. One of the British ships was shooting at the redoubt on Breed's Hill. Gage called a meeting, or council of war. Gage, Howe, Clinton, and Burgoyne knew that if the Americans finished the redoubt and put cannons in it, they could harm British ships in the harbor.

The four generals agreed that they needed to attack. The only questions were where and how. The soldiers would have to move by boat from Boston. They had only 28 boats. The boats could carry about 1,500 men. That was too few men to begin an attack. So the boats would have to return to Boston to get more men. The tides would influence the timing of these movements.

On the night of June 16, 1775, rebel forces built a fortification on Breed's Hill. The British attacked the next day, June 17, 1775. The rebels beat off two British charges. A third finally drove the Americans from Breed's Hill. Named after nearby Bunker Hill, the battle was a costly British victory.

breastworks: piles of dirt or wood quickly put up to protect soldiers on a battlefield

The generals had to think about all of this. They decided to land at Moulton Point. The point was safe from rebel fire coming from Breed's Hill. The British would then split into two groups. One group would take position, or deploy, in front of Breed's Hill. Its job was to attract the rebels' attention. Meanwhile, the main group would then march west past Breed's Hill toward Bunker Hill. In other words, they would outflank the American defenders on Breed's Hill. If the plan worked, the rebels would be trapped with no way to retreat. General Howe took command of the attack. General Gage remained in Boston.

While the British generals made plans, the Royal Navy bombarded the rebels. One of the first shots tore the head off Private Asa Pollard as he worked in front of the redoubt. Colonel William Prescott later wrote, "He was so near me that my clothes were [splattered] with his blood and brains." The first casualty shocked the militia. Men gathered to stare at the body. They felt their stomachs turn over because they saw that death could

A view of the Charlestown Peninsula where the battle took place.

Above: Colonel John Stark was a combat veteran of great experience. To help his men know when to shoot, he set a mark on the beach fifty yards in front of his men. He told them not to fire until the British passed this mark. He was an outstanding leader and one of the heroes of the Battle of Bunker Hill.

happen to anyone. Some became so afraid that they went to the rear to find safety.

When General Ward learned that the British boats were moving toward Charlestown, he decided to send reinforcements. The result was confusion. Again the lack of American staff officers made things difficult. Some regiments advanced smartly onto the Charlestown Peninsula. Others milled about while the men debated what to do. After all, the militia were not used to taking orders, particularly from men who were their friends and neighbors. Some soldiers were simply too scared to march onto the peninsula. In one case a captain ordered his men to advance and said he would join them shortly. The men never saw him again that day.

Meanwhile, the first wave of British troops landed at Moulton Point. It was about 2 P.M. on a warm, clear day.

The rebel commander was Colonel Prescott. Prescott saw that the British planned to march past his left (northern) flank. There was a 200-yard-wide gap beyond Prescott's left. Prescott ordered an artillery officer to take two guns to plug the gap. He told a Connecticut captain named Thomas Knowlton to take his 200 men and support the cannons.

The artillery officer proved a coward. He ignored his orders and led his men to the rear. Captain Knowlton was an intelligent and brave leader. He calmly looked around. He decided the best thing to do was to occupy a stone and rail fence about 200 yards to the left rear of Breed's Hill.

Other rebel units were moving to reinforce Prescott. They had to march across a narrow neck of land. British gunboats fired cannons to try to stop them. Captain Henry Dearborn suggested that the men run through the danger zone. Colonel John Stark of New Hampshire replied, "one fresh man in action is worth ten fatigued men." So the rebels marched slowly through the fire.

Stark saw that Knowlton's position was important. He led his men to join Knowlton. Stark also saw that there was still a gap on Knowlton's left, just along the edge of

the Mystic River. So Stark sent some men to plug that gap as well.

Another group of Americans marched up Bunker Hill. Colonel Israel Putnam was there. He tried to take charge and ordered them to begin digging trenches. Some men listened. Others did not recognize Putnam as their leader. They stood confused and waited to see what would happen.

Two other famous patriots entered the battle around this time. Seth Pomeroy was a 69-year-old veteran. He was a gunsmith by profession and had helped train the Massachusetts militia. On this day Pomeroy carried a musket he had made himself and used during the French and Indian War. The other famous patriot was Dr. Joseph Warren, the president of the Massachusetts Provincial Congress. Both Pomeroy and Warren refused a position of command. Instead, both wanted to serve in the front ranks with the privates.

Below: British reinforcements cross the water while Royal Navy ships bombard the American position. Charlestown is burning.

Pomeroy joined Stark's men at the fence. Warren went to the redoubt on Breed's Hill.

By the time the American reinforcements arrived, the second British wave landed. General Howe looked through his telescope to study the rebel position. It looked strong. But Howe knew that his men were professional soldiers and that the rebels were not. Howe sent for more reinforcements and ordered his men to eat lunch.

American marksmen had been shooting at the British from the shelter of Charlestown. Howe ordered the artillery and ships to open fire and drive them out. The

Knowlton's men wait for the British grenadiers to come closer before opening fire. An officer told the militia, "Do not fire until you see the whites of their eyes!"

bombardment set the buildings on fire. A thick cloud of smoke rose.

Howe decided to begin his attack after the third wave of British soldiers arrived. The first collision came at the fence defended by Stark and the New Hampshire men. Eleven companies of light infantry advanced quickly along the beach. Stark told his men to aim low and aim at the officers. The rebels waited until the light infantry were only fifty yards away. Then Stark ordered them to fire.

The first volley slaughtered the nearest British soldiers. The soldiers in the rear bravely pushed forward through their fallen comrades. Stark had organized his men in three ranks. While one rank fired, the others reloaded. In that way the militia kept up a never-ending fire.

The light infantry could not stand the fire. They retreated. Ninety-six dead soldiers were left on the narrow beach. They lay so thick that they reminded one American of sheep in a pen.

The first British effort had failed. Next, Howe personally led his grenadiers in an attack against the fence defended by Knowlton's men. Before the attack Israel Putnam had joined Knowlton's militia. He walked among them shouting out words of encouragement. Knowlton's men waited until the grenadiers were fifty yards away before shooting. They too aimed at the officers.

The grenadiers were supposed to ignore this fire and charge with their bayonets. But Knowlton's fire forced the grenadiers to halt. They fired back at the militia. Since the rebels were behind cover and the grenadiers were in the open, it was not an equal fight. The colonel commanding the grenadiers received a mortal wound. Many other grenadiers were hit. After a short time the grenadiers retreated.

The British regrouped for about fifteen minutes. Then Howe and General Robert Pigot led them forward again. This time the main British attack went in against the left of Breed's Hill. At the same time, the light infantry tried again to charge Knowlton and Stark. The rebels had piled fence rails to make three fleches, V-shaped defenses with their point toward the enemy, to the left of the redoubt. If the British captured the fleches, they would outflank the redoubt.

Once the fighting became hand-to-hand, the British bayonets gave the redcoats the advantage.

Once more the rebels held their fire until the British came very close. A British officer described what happened: "As we approached, [a continuous] stream of fire poured from the rebel lines; it seemed a continued sheet of fire for near 30 minutes...Most of our Grenadiers and Light-infantry...lost three-fourths, and many nine-tenths of their men. Some had only eight and nine men a company left, some only three, four, and five."

Untrained American militia had twice driven back the best soldiers in the world. But now they were running very low on ammunition. On the other hand, the British had received a third wave of reinforcements. General Clinton also crossed the water to join the attack.

Howe ordered a third attack. This time he used his artillery. It moved into position to fire against fleches and the rear of the breastworks on Breed's Hill. At the same time, Major Pitcairn, the officer who had led the advance to Lexington and Concord, moved against the American right. Howe, Pigot, and Clinton led the rest of the infantry straight up the hill.

The people of Boston watch the battle from the rooftops on Copp's Hill.

The rebels fought hard. They fired volley after volley at point-blank range. John Pitcairn fell with a mortal wound. Many other redcoats were hit. The British bravely climbed over the earthworks and entered the rebel redoubt. A wild hand-to-hand fight took place.

One Rhode Island soldier had a type of sword known as a cutlass. Although it was old, dull, and rust-eaten, it saved his life: "A blow with a cutlass was aimed at my head by a British officer, which I parried [blocked], and received only a slight cut with the point to my right arm." The Rhode Islander swung back and cut off the British officer's arm. He proudly reported, "with one well directed stroke I deprived him the power of very soon again measuring swords with a 'yankee rebel'!"

In the redoubt the British had the advantage of their 14-inch bayonets. Only a few of the militia had bayonets. Instead, they used their muskets like clubs and threw rocks. This was a fight the rebels could not win. The redcoats bayoneted 30 rebels to death inside the redoubt, including Dr. Warren.

The surviving patriots fell back. Corporal Amos Farnsworth wrote how he was retreating when "I received a wound in my right arm, the ball going through a little below my elbow, breaking the little bone. Another ball struck my back, taking a piece of skin about as big as a penny....Oh, the goodness of God in preserving my life."

General John Burgoyne was in Boston watching the fight. He reported that the American "retreat was no rout." The British chased the defeated rebels. Although some rebels ran in panic, many kept up a running fight from fence to wall all of the way back past Bunker Hill.

The fighting raged on the slopes of Breed's Hill.

Because they were out of ammunition, some men threw rocks at the charging British.

So the battle, which took place on Breed's Hill but which history remembers as the Battle of Bunker Hill, ended. The British claimed victory because they had driven off the rebels. They had also captured Breed's Hill and Bunker Hill.

The number of rebels who fought at Bunker Hill is unknown. It is certain that the Americans outnumbered the British. The number of American casualties is also not known. At least 115 were killed and another 305 wounded. The British suffered far more, losing at least 1,150. The loss among officers was particularly heavy. General Clinton called it "a dear bought victory, another such would have ruined us."

For the British Bunker Hill was the bloodiest battle of the war. Almost a full year would pass before the British attacked the rebels anywhere again. Never again would a British general act so quickly and boldly. Bunker Hill had taught the British caution.

For the Americans Bunker Hill taught the rebels that they could fight and win against the redcoats. The presence of veteran leaders such as Prescott, Putnam, Knowlton, and Stark had been invaluable. They knew how to command militia. They understood that their citizen-soldiers would fight best if they were fighting from behind cover. The battle also showed American leaders that there was little real hope of peace.

Chronology

December 16, 1773: The Boston Tea Party takes place. Boston radicals dump tea into Boston Harbor to protest against taxes on tea.

June 1, 1774: To punish the people of Boston for the Boston Tea Party, England passes a set of laws that closes the port of Boston and puts the city under martial law, or military rule. The Americans call the laws the Intolerable Acts.

September 1774: In response to the Intolerable Acts the First Continental Congress meets in Philadelphia.

April 18–19, 1775: Paul Revere makes his famous ride to alert the countryside that the British army regulars are on the move. He is captured by the British after he has spread the alarm.

April 19, 1775: The Battle of Lexington and Concord, the first battle of the American Revolution.

May 10, 1775: The Second Continental Congress gathers in Philadelphia.

May 10, 1775: Ethan Allen and the Green Mountain Boys capture Fort Ticonderoga, New York, without a fight.

June 14, 1775: The Second Continental Congress votes to create the Continental Army.

June 15, 1775: The Second Continental Congress elects George Washington to command the Continental Army.

June 17, 1775: The Battle of Bunker Hill.

Glossary

ARTILLERY: a group of cannons and other large guns used to help an army by firing, or shooting, at enemy troops

BAYONET: a sword attached to the muzzle of a musket or rifle

BREASTWORKS: piles of dirt or wood quickly put up to protect soldiers on a battlefield

BRIGADE: an army unit made up of four or more regiments. Three or more brigades make up a division.

CASUALTIES: people killed, wounded, captured, or missing after a battle

COLUMN: a narrow, deep formation where soldiers stand in many ranks behind the front rank. The most common column is a road column in which the front rank is as wide as the road, and the rest of the soldiers march behind the front rank.

COMPANY: a small army unit numbering 25 to 50 men. Ten companies make up a regiment.

COUNCIL OF WAR: a meeting of officers to decide on how to fight

DEPLOY: to arrange forces for a battle; also to move from one formation, such as a column, into another, such as a line

DESERT: to leave the army or navy without permission

DISARM: to take away weapons by force

DRILL: to practice firing weapons and maneuvering (including deploying from column to line and from line to column)

FIRE DISCIPLINE: the ability to fire only when ordered during a battle

GARRISON: the group of soldiers stationed at a fort or military post

GRENADIER: a member of a special, or elite, group of infantry soldiers

INFANTRY: foot soldiers, or soldiers who march and fight on foot

LIGHT INFANTRY: a special, or elite, group of foot soldiers chosen for its ability to move and think quickly

LINE: a long, shallow formation two or three ranks deep; the typical battle formation since it lets all the soldiers fire their muskets

MILITIA: a group of citizens not normally part of the army that mobilizes for the purpose of defending the homeland in an emergency; also used as a plural to describe several such groups

MINUTEMEN: a special militia organized in Massachusetts, so called for its ability to gather in a few minutes

MUSKET: a smoothbore, single-shot gun used by foot soldiers in battle. Muskets were not as accurate as rifles.

OUTFLANK: to move around the side, or flank, of the enemy troops on a battlefield

PATRIOT: an American who wanted the colonies to be independent of the British Empire; from patriotic, which means devoted to the good of one's country

PLATOON: a small group of foot soldiers

POINT-BLANK: at very close range; refers to the firing of a shot

PROPAGANDA: information presented in a way to convince people of a certain point of view

PROVINCIAL: of the provinces, or colonies

RANK: a line or row of soldiers, as in front rank; also an official position within the military such as private, captain, or general

RATIONS: food and drink issued to soldiers

REDCOATS: British soldiers, who typically wore a uniform with a red coat

REDOUBT: a temporary stronghold or fortification often built in front of the main position

REGIMENT: an army unit made up of ten companies. A regiment at full strength had about 450 soldiers.

REGROUP: to assemble again after being broken apart by the actions of a battle

REGULARS: professional soldiers who belong to the army full time

ROUT: a disorderly retreat, or panicked flight from the battlefield

SMOOTHBORE: having no grooves inside the barrel (of a gun). Such grooves make a gun shoot more accurately.

STAFF: soldiers assigned to help officers make plans and carry out the plans

TACTICS: the science and art of positioning and using soldiers or ships in battle

VOLLEY: the firing of a group of guns at the same time

About the Authors

James R. Arnold has written more than 20 books on military history topics and contributed to many others. Roberta Wiener has coauthored several books with Mr. Arnold and edited numerous educational books, including a children's encyclopedia. They live and farm in Virginia.

Further Resources

Books:

Bliven, Bruce, Jr. *The American Revolution.* New York: Random House, 1986.

Brenner, Barbara. *If You Were There in 1776.* New York: Bradbury Press, 1994. Details of daily life in the rebellious colonies in 1776.

Dolan, Edward F. *The American Revolution: How We Fought the War of Independence.* Brookfield, CT: Millbrook Press, 1995.

Forbes, Esther. *Paul Revere and the World He Lived In.* Boston: Houghton Mifflin, Co., 1999.

Johnson, Neil. *The Battle of Lexington and Concord.* New York: Four Winds Press, 1992.

King, David. *Lexington & Concord.* New York: 21st Century Books, 1997.

Murphy, Jim. *A Young Patriot: The American Revolution as Experienced by One Boy.* New York: Clarion Books, 1996. Based on the life story of a real person, Joseph Plumb Martin, who was 15 years old when he enlisted in the Continental Army.

Russell, Francis. *Lexington, Concord and Bunker Hill.* New York: American Heritage Publishing Co., 1963.

Websites:

http://library.thinkquest.org/10966/
The Revolutionary War—A Journey Towards Freedom

ushistory.org/march/index.html
Virtual Marching Tour of the American Revolution

http://www.pbs.org/ktca/liberty/game/index.html
The Road to Revolution—A Revolutionary Game

http://www.pbs.org/ktca/liberty/chronicle/index.html
Chronicle of the Revolution
Read virtual newspapers of the Revolutionary era

http://www.vboston.com/VBoston/Content/FreedomTrail/Index.cfm

http://www.concordma.com/history.html

Places to Visit:

Fort Ticonderoga Museum, Ticonderoga, New York

Minuteman National Historical Park, Concord, Massachusetts

Set Index

Bold numbers refer to volumes; *italics* refer to illustrations

Acknowledgments

Author's collection: 14T, 16B
Anne S. K. Brown Military Collection, John Hay Library, Brown University, Providence, Rhode Island: 8–9,
  40–41, 62, 66
Architect of the Capitol: 42–43, 44–45, 45
Charles C. Coffin, *Boys of '76*, 1876, 26T, 27T
Eldridge S. Brooks, *The Century Book of the American Revolution*, 1897, 25T, 27B
Harper's New Monthly Magazine: 10T, 11
Harper's Weekly: 63
Independence National Historical Park: 7, 16T
Library of Congress: Title page, 14–15, 18, 19T, 24–25, 32, 33T, 33B, 34, 38, 43, 53
Military Archive & Research Services, England: 29T
National Archives: 10B, 12–13, 17, 19B, 20, 21, 22, 23, 25B, 26B, 29B, 35, 46–47, 50, 51, 52T, 52B, 57,
  58, 59T, 59B
National Guard Bureau: 30–31 a National Guard Heritage Painting by Don Troiani, 60–61
National Park Service: 36–37 *First Blood of the Revolutionary War*, painting by John Rush, photography by
  Michael Tropea, Chicago
U.S. Government Printing Office: 6, 47, 64–65
Henry C. Watson, *Campfires of the Revolution*, 1858, 55
West Point Museum Collection, United States Military Academy: Front cover, Title page, 39, 54 photographed by
  Anthony Mario, Gateway Studio, Fishkill, NY

Maps by Jerry Malone